ACCLAIM FOR ANDREA KIHLSTEDT'S

How to Raise $1 Million (or More!)
in 10 Bite-Sized Steps

"If you're raising money to make the world a better place, turn off
your computer for an hour and read this bool̲
a fun read, *How to Raise A Million Dollars f*
most in fundraising – human nature."

> *Larry Eason*, Board Chair
> Healthy Child Healthy W₍

"This book is at once simple and brilliant. Take the passion you ha͞v͞
for your organization and overlay these essential fundraising steps.
You're sure to have a successful campaign."

> *Rosalyn Ward*, Campaign Manager
> Central Market Campaign

"Andrea Kihlstedt already knows your organization. She knows your
strengths, limitations, fears, phobias and conceits. You will see
yourself on every page. It is a little eerie."

> *Jim Bunting*, Founder
> The Science Factory

"Andrea Kihlstedt's book will inspire you to learn both the theory and
how, in practice, to make it possible. STEP 1 for anyone contemplating
a major gifts campaign should be: Buy this book."

> *Jethro Miller,* Vice President
> American Red Cross, National Campaign

"How to Raise $1 Million is important reading for all of us who
bravely move ahead despite many uncertainties."

> *Mary Sylvester,* Director of Alumni Relations and
> University Advancement
> University of Maine at Farmington

"*Bite-Sized Steps* brings to life real stories about how ordinary people
step up and do extraordinary things in order to make a difference in the
world."

> *Tomijean Fernandez,* Director, Affiliate Training
> Affiliate Support Department, ACLU

ANDREA KIHLSTEDT

How to **Raise**

$1 Million

(or More!)

in **10**

Bite-Sized Steps

A FAIL-PROOF GUIDE
for Board Members, Volunteers and Staff

Emerson
& Church
PUBLISHERS

First printed in January 2010

Printed in the United States of America

ISBN 978-1-889102-41-2

10 9 8 7 6 5 4 3 2 1

This text is printed on acid-free paper.

*Copies of this book are available from the
publisher at discount when purchased in
quantity for boards of directors or staff.*

Emerson & Church, Publishers
28A Park Street • Medfield, MA 02052
Tel. 508-359-0019 • www.emersonandchurch.com

Library of Congress Cataloging-in-Publication Data

Kihlstedt, Andrea.
  How to raise a million dollars (or more!) in 10 bite-sized
steps : a failproof guide for board members, volunteers, and
staff / by Andrea Kihlstedt.
     p. cm.
  ISBN 978-1-889102-41-2 (pbk. : alk. paper)
  1. Fund raising. 2. Nonprofit organizations—Finance. 3.
Charities—Finance. I. Title.
  HG177.K513 2010
  658.15'224—dc22
                              2009039140

For Tyko, with whom I walk through life.

Companion Books

Fund Raising Realities
Every Board Member Must Face
A 1-Hour Crash Course on Raising
Major Gifts for Nonprofit Organizations
David Lansdowne

If every board member of every nonprofit organization across America read this book, it's no exaggeration to say that millions upon millions of additional dollars would be raised.

How could it be otherwise when, after spending just *one* hour with this gem, board members everywhere would understand virtually everything they need to know about raising major gifts.

David Lansdowne distills the essence of major gifts fundraising, puts it in the context of 47 "realities," and delivers it all in unfailingly clear prose.

Among the *Top Three* bestselling fundraising books of all time.

ASKING
A 59-Minute Guide to Everything
Board Members, Volunteers, and Staff
Must Know to Secure the Gift
Jerold Panas

It ranks right up there with public speaking. Nearly all of us fear it. And yet it's critical to the success of our organizations. Asking for money. It makes even the stout-hearted quiver.

But now comes a book, *Asking,* and short of a medical elixir, it's the next best thing for emboldening board members, volunteers, and staff to ask with skill, finesse ... and powerful results.

What *Asking* convincingly shows is that it doesn't take stellar sales skills to be an effective asker. Nearly everyone, regardless of their persuasive ability, can become an effective fundraiser if they follow Panas' step-by-step guidelines.

Emerson & Church, Publishers
www.emersonandchurch.com

"One step at a time is good walking."

–Chinese Proverb

Every story I tell in this book is real...

But it would violate an unspoken trust if I were to reveal certain names and organizations. So I've taken care to conceal the identity of some.

During my 27 years as a capital campaign consultant, I've had countless opportunities to observe volunteers and staff at their best – rising to meet seemingly impossible challenges. I've also encountered times when, despite their best intentions, individuals have lost their moorings.

It is these moments that unveil the true insights of fundraising and enliven this book.

INTRODUCTION

A million dollars!

Is that a lot of money?

The answer depends on where you stand – or sit.

For some, it's an unthinkably large sum. For others, it's a small blip on their radar screen.

In writing this book, I use $1 million as a placeholder. A symbol of whatever amount you need to raise. The 10 steps I outline will work whether you're raising $10,000 for your child's school ... a million for a new day care center ... five million for your local library ... or 100 million for your college.

The timetable and complexity of the process will vary, of course. But if you follow these 10 essential steps *in the right order*, the chances are good you will succeed.

They've worked for both well-established organizations and start-ups. They've worked for organizations like the YWCA, Boys and Girls Club, Planned Parenthood, theater groups, schools and churches. They've worked for Cornell University and

Skidmore College.

These 10 steps don't work because they're magic – though it sometimes feels that way. They work because they're based on *an understanding of how most people function*. In fact, observing people throughout my career – first as a philosopher, then working in urban development, and finally as a fundraising consultant who specialized in difficult and unlikely projects – I've become convinced there are *rules* for human behavior. They are:

- People want to share in success
- People are consistent
- We must give before we can ask others
- With involvement comes investment

It's not easy to develop an organized fundraising system that incorporates all of these principles – but fortunately, you don't have to!

This book does the job for you, outlining a step-by-step process for raising money that makes use of these basic human behaviors and motivations.

That's the reason this method has worked for so many successful nonprofits. And that's why it will work for you!

I wish you well with your fundraising and send you my great appreciation for all of your work to make your community and our world a better place.

Bronx, New York   *Andrea Kihlstedt*

CONTENTS

STEP 1

Inspire Goosebumps

Willis ran the largest foundation in town. And he knew goosebumps. In fact, unless he felt goosebumps about a project, he wasn't likely to fund it, at least with any big money. And he wasn't feeling his skin tingle as he listened to Jim.

As a child, Jim had trouble reading and struggled through school. He was super-smart and unendingly curious, but book learning just didn't come easily. In spite of – or perhaps because of – his early struggles, Jim grew up to be a successful advertising executive. But he always remembered that awful sense of feeling dumb in school.

Many years later when Jim retired, he decided to create a place where young people could learn differently – a science center where kids would be encouraged to play and experiment and work from their own curiosity rather than be spoonfed in the classroom.

Jim consulted with various advisors and educators and set up the legal structure for his Science Factory. But when he set about raising $1 million to get the organization up and running, it didn't take him long to realize that not everyone got goosebumps when they thought about different ways of learning. In fact, very few people understood the importance of alternative learning opportunities at all.

So here he was sitting across from Willis. A gift from Willis' foundation was critical if Jim wanted to establish credibility for his project.

When Jim finished laying out his vision, Willis stood up and adjusted his glasses. "I don't get it," he said. "Why do we need an entire science center for a few kids who aren't smart enough to do well in school?"

That's when Jim knew he had a big problem! His passion for supporting alternative learning styles wasn't shared by Willis. He knew he'd have a hard time seeing Willis again, so almost instantly Jim, a very resourceful thinker, switched to Plan B. Instead of talking about learning disabilities, he turned the discussion to the poor science scores in the local school district.

Willis' ears perked up.

Then Jim told Willis that the new building would draw more than 40,000 people downtown each year.

Willis' ears perked up even more.

These issues were pertinent to the entire community, and that made them far more important to Willis than alternative learning styles, the issue fueling Jim's passions.

In the end, Willis' foundation gave $150,000 which got the Science Factory off the ground and established credibility for the project.

And Jim learned a critical lesson: that he had to approach different people in different ways, ways that reflected their particular interests and passions and inspired a real connection of the goosebump variety.

■ Applying your insights

Jim's experience points up the importance of *understanding why our fundraising projects matter to the people we're asking to give.*

As Jim discovered, every donor gives for his or her own reasons. And early on, Jim had to think through the many reasons people might give, so that he could explain exactly how *his* project intersected with *their* interests. In doing so, Jim not only began to articulate a compelling case for the Science Factory, he also expanded his thinking about the *kinds* of people who might give.

Based on his new thinking, Jim now knew how to approach:

• Sam, an inventor who wanted to give children a chance to tinker and explore

• Judy, a teacher who hungered for more chances for her students to learn about science

• Bill, who had worked for years to attract more tourists downtown, and believed Jim's Science Factory would help him meet that goal, and

• Anne, who wanted a place to bring her grandchildren on rainy days.

All of these people who might not have donated to an "alternative learning experience" gave generously to the Science Factory when Jim was able to show them how it supported their own particular passions.

■ How do you bridge the gap?

So how do you do what Jim was forced to do on the spot? How do you take your organization's needs and turn them into a donor's dream? It's not so hard, really. It simply means thinking from the outside in.

In other words, you need to view your organization not from the nuts-and-bolts perspective central to *your* life, but from the point of view of potential donors. Which of your programs might overlap with their specific interests?

Ask yourself this critical question: What will we be able to accomplish in the community when our project is completed? To answer that, you'll need to delve a little deeper: Who will benefit and in what ways? Will our services improve? Will we deliver *more* services? Whose lives will be changed, and how? How will the community be stronger?

Let's look at another example.

Ralph heads up the Lancaster County Conservancy. Lancaster County is known far and wide for the many Amish farms located there.

The mission of Ralph's organization is to preserve forested land in the region, constituting about 15 percent of the county. The importance of these areas is less apparent than farmland but every bit as compelling.

As Ralph spoke to people in the community, he found they fell into two categories: those who are naturally drawn to the outdoors – the campers, fishermen, hunters and hikers – and those who aren't. For the outdoor types, the case was obvious. These people benefit directly from having forests and trails and clean streams and creeks practically in their backyard.

But Ralph found that his organization also speaks

to those who aren't outdoors types. They paid attention when he spoke of the effect of the Conservancy on their health and their pocketbooks.

Ralph could show that the forestland his organization protects leads directly to clean water and air. He could also document that more protected forestland leads to higher real estate values. And the higher the quality of the environment, the more businesses and employees would be drawn to the county, resulting in a stronger economy. Paradoxically, the faster the economic growth, the more need for the Lancaster County Conservancy.

By listening to people in the community, Ralph, like Jim, was able to tap into what was most important to them. And in doing so he laid the groundwork for them to become staunch supporters of the Conservancy.

■ One last thought

Jim, of the Science Factory, likes to tell the story of a man named Joe, who went to his favorite lake to fish. In the morning, Joe used crickets as bait, but had no luck. So in the afternoon, he switched to worms.

Toward dusk, a friend of Joe's came by. When he saw that Joe hadn't caught a single fish all day, the friend asked him what he was using for bait.

"In the morning, crickets," said Joe, "and in the afternoon, worms."

Without warning, Joe's friend plunged his face into the water and shouted to the fish, "What do you like for bait?"

"Try Cheese Whiz," they replied.

STEP 2

Set a Breathtaking Goal

Terry, the founder and artistic director of the Arden Theatre Company, decided it was time to create a main stage theatre.

A few years earlier, he'd raised money to renovate a small commercial space in Philadelphia's historic Old City neighborhood. But after three successful seasons, his company was having growing pains, and Terry decided to raise money again, this time for a larger, more flexible theatre.

He began his new fundraising process with STEP 1 – talking and talking to people about his vision, to find out what struck *them* as compelling.

In the course of these conversations, Terry found

that many were excited about his basic plan. But again and again people bemoaned the lack of professional theatre *for children* in the Philadelphia region. They asked if the new performance space would be big enough to support a children's theater program.

STEP 1 gave Terry key information about what people wanted. Ultimately, he decided to add the cost of starting and operating a new children's theatre program to his fundraising goals. He also added an endowment fund to help with building maintenance, the costs for fundraising, and a healthy amount for contingencies.

These additions increased his initial goal of $2 million to $3.5 million. And, as Terry's goal grew, so did the breadth and appeal of his project.

Of course, finding an additional $1.5 million wasn't easy. Although the addition of the children's theatre did bring in some new donors, it also required a great deal more fundraising and a considerable amount of work to create a tenable plan for this new aspect of the program.

For 18 months, Terry and his gang worked like mad. In the theatre world, one gets used to long hours and late nights, but adding this expanded campaign on top of the normal rigors of the performing arts field upped the stress level even farther.

Albeit exhausted, Terry did in the end succeed in raising $3.5 million – a breathtaking goal compared to the $2 million originally sought. Expanding a campaign mid-stream isn't wise for everyone, but it worked in this case. Now, several years later, when I take my grandchildren to a play at the Arden, I see the wonderful results.

■ The steps are the same

As you think about financing the vision for your organization, you may be surprised to discover that, rather than thinking small, your best bet is to begin by thinking big!

Why?

Because raising $1.5 million is usually no more difficult than raising $1 million. In either case, you'll go through the same process and approach the very same donors. The difference is only one of scale.

This sounds strange, I know. But often the same person who can afford to contribute $100,000 can also give you $250,000 if she's convinced the larger expenditure will make the project notably stronger.

For example, when Morrow House decided to renovate its theatre, the board budgeted conservatively and set out to raise $750,000. They did succeed in raising the money and renovating the space, but because they were pinching pennies, they didn't replace the seats in the theatre – a $120,000 item.

When the campaign's largest donor came to the ribbon cutting, he was appalled. His name was on the plaque in the newly renovated theatre but everyone was sitting on lumpy, worn seats. He felt it reflected poorly on him, and would much rather have added another $120,000 to his gift if only he'd been asked. After the fact, he felt he had no choice but to come up with the money for the seats. But that second gift, while given graciously, was colored by a sense of obligation rather than a sense of joy.

The risks of thinking big early in the process are few, and the rewards may be great. You'll have a chance later to scale back if your goal proves untenable. But you won't have a second chance to set bigger goals or create a broader vision once your campaign is underway.

That's why you'll begin STEP 2 by considering *all* the costs you may incur to bring your project to fruition.

For the moment, let's imagine your goal is to purchase and renovate a building that'll serve as your organization's new home. Beyond the basic costs – buying the structure, purchasing materials for the renovation, paying contractor's fees and labor – think about additional factors such as:

⟨•⟩ How much will it cost to relocate your programs?

⟨•⟩ Will you incur extraordinary costs to get those programs up and running at the new site? Will you need new staff? Or perhaps more computers? Will the security system be adequate?

⟨•⟩ Are there other aspects of your operations that, if improved now, would greatly benefit your entire program? Might you, for example, need an upgraded telephone system that would make scheduling easier and more efficient?

⟨•⟩ Would it be wise to consider raising your endowment so that it will cover the costs of maintaining the building over the long term?

And don't forget to include a line in your budget to cover the cost of fundraising. Even the most modest fundraising effort will cost *something*, and you'd be wise to budget for it.

Lastly, add a healthy contingency amount to your goal – perhaps as much as 10 percent – to cover the unanticipated costs you're bound to incur. In my experience, even the most rigorous budgeters don't anticipate everything.

As you begin to assemble the specifics for your budget, you'll probably find you need to raise more money than you originally thought. Your goal may actually *double* by the time you've added up all the numbers.

But even if you've reached for the sky, which I don't necessarily recommend, you'll be able to reality-check your goal before making it public. We'll get to that before long.

STEP 3

Develop a By-the-Numbers Plan

Four years after opening its doors, the Janus School, an independent day school, was fast outgrowing its leased space. The board decided to raise money to buy land and build a new school. They found a piece of land, hired an architect, and developed their plans.

Looking at all of the costs, the board figured they'd need approximately $1 million. It was their great good fortune that the builder had children at the school and could shave a good bit off the costs.

The big challenge was the size of their community. When the board made a list of potential donors – even adding grandparents, area foundations, teachers, board members and, of course, parents – they could only come up with a list of fewer than 250 people, total.

How, they wondered, could they raise $1 million from such a limited pool?

With the help of a consultant, the board drew up what's called a Table of Gifts, a commonly used fundraising tool showing how many donors are needed at what levels of giving to achieve a desired goal.

Before I share their table with you, let me reiterate something you already know. Wealth isn't evenly distributed in our society: some are rich, others are poor, and many are somewhere in between.

Effective fundraising reflects this pattern. To raise $1 million, you'll need a few big gifts, more middle size gifts, and lots of little ones.

What decades of experience have shown is the following:

• *Most fundraising campaigns require one gift that totals 15 to 20 percent of the goal.* This one gift sets the bar and others will give in proportion to it.

• In most campaigns, *the top 10 gifts will comprise at least half of the goal.*

If you can raise the 10 gifts that get you over the halfway mark, the rest is likely to fall into place, because these gifts create a sense of inevitability, and build confidence in other donors that your project will be successful.

When board members of the Janus School sat down to figure out how they were going to raise so much money from such a limited pool, it became clear at once that they'd need a few extraordinary gifts from a handful of exceptionally generous people.

They also saw that unlike most campaigns, there was no room for error. There were only a few people in town who could make the kind of gifts the school needed.

Here's what the Janus's Table of Gifts looked like:

JANUS SCHOOL'S NEW BUILDING PROJECT
Table of Gifts

# GIFTS	AMOUNT	TOTAL GIVEN	CUMULATIVE TOTAL
1	$250,000	$250,000	$250,000
2	$100,000	$200,000	$450,000
4	$50,000	$200,000	$650,000
8	$25,000	$200,000	$850,000
10	$10,000	$100,000	$950,000
200	<$10,000	$50,000	$1,000,000

As you can see, the school needed to depend on a whopping FOUR! people to reach half of its goal. If the board couldn't identify individuals within the immediate community with both the ability and the inclination to make gifts of that size, they'd have to abandon their plans. Otherwise, they'd be tilting at windmills.

Undaunted, a small group of staff and board members began reviewing the school's extended family. They winnowed it down to a small number of potential donors. At the same time, they began talking with some of the wealthiest parents and grandparents to see if they were willing to take a large stake in the new school. They showed each person the Table of Gifts.

When one set of grandparents agreed to make the top gift and to ask some of the other families to consider large gifts, it seemed as if the campaign had a good chance to succeed.

Still, the effort was continually fraught with anxiety. Nearly every prospective donor required many conversations. One gift, for example, was made to honor a woman who had passed away the year before. She was the grandmother of one of the school's students. As you would expect, decisions around this gift were made by various family members and everyone had a different idea of the amount and how it should be made. Since this gift was pivotal – the campaign was doomed without it – securing it felt like a high stakes venture. But, then again, so did every one of the other sizable gifts.

Fundraising of this sort, when the pool of donors

is so constricted, isn't for the impatient or the faint of heart. It takes huge will, lots of energy, and the ability to function strategically.

■ A versatile tool

For the Janus School, more than 90 percent of the funds had to come from 10 percent of people identified. For other groups with larger donor pools, the ratio might be a more comfortable 80-20 or even 70-30.

The pattern underpinning the Table of Gifts is somewhat mathematical, but the exact formula you use will grow out of your understanding of your organization, your community, and your donor base. A more common and less stressful pattern would show a donor base that's large enough to line up four or five prospects for every anticipated gift.

But the Table of Gifts isn't just a road map. It's also a mirror, a conversation piece, and a yardstick. As you tinker with the numbers, notice how quickly you identify where *your own gift* fits on the chart.

You'll also find that everyone you show it to experiences the same reaction! The Table is like a mirror, reflecting back our ability to give.

It's also a wonderful conversation starter when you're actually soliciting gifts. The Table defines possible gift levels in an objective, non-threatening way.

I remember Barbara, a wonderful volunteer and donor who was willing to solicit her friend Charles for the hospice in her community, even though she was truly uncomfortable talking about money.

The idea of asking her friend for a gift of a specific amount made Barbara almost nauseous. The development director thought Charles had the capacity to give $50,000, but he knew Barbara would be incapable of asking for that. So instead, he sent her off with a Table of Gifts that had the $50,000 level highlighted.

When Barbara sat down with Charles, she didn't have to say anything about the size of the gift. All she had to do was to place the chart in front of him (which in itself was still difficult for Barbara). Charles could see that $50,000 wasn't the largest gift but was still in the top group. He looked at Barbara and said, "So this is where you think I fit." Barbara nodded nervously. "You're right," he said! And that was that.

One last thing about the Table of Gifts. In addition to the other uses I mentioned, it's also a yardstick for progress. As gifts come in, you can literally check them off, showing donors in a very specific and visual way how your fundraising is progressing. That reinforces their confidence in you and very well could lead to additional gifts from friends and colleagues of theirs.

■ Trust the pattern

Sometimes it's hard for people to accept that the best way to raise money is this pattern of a few large gifts, a few more mid-size gifts, and lots of smaller ones.

I recently worked on a project to raise $1 million to renovate a community market building that's home to many local businesses.

In an early planning meeting, Art, one of the more powerful committee members, said he was convinced the best way to raise half of the money was to get 500 people to each give a thousand dollars.

"After all," Art reasoned, "the market is the heart of the community and hundreds of thousands of people shop here every year. Why should a few people bear the brunt of this fundraising?" Art suggested we sell 500 paving bricks at a thousand dollars each. "We'll raise half of the money that way and be done by the end of the summer," he concluded.

Sounds deceptively easy and logical, except for one fatal flaw. People – and count yourself among them – aren't inclined to write checks of a thousand dollars without being carefully cultivated and solicited. Art's idea was simply impractical. We had neither the staff nor the time nor the resources to identify, cultivate, and sell bricks to 500 people.

Oh, yes, there was another (big) problem as well.

People who patronized the market didn't think of it as a nonprofit. To them, it was a wonderful public space where they shopped, and the fact that the city owned the building made it all the more difficult to raise private money. To get *anyone* to make a significant gift was going to take a lot of personal attention and energy. And we certainly weren't able to do that on any large scale.

Many months later, when the fundraising drew to a successful close, it turned out that the gifts we received reflected the pattern of wealth in the community. A small number of people made large gifts, a larger number made mid-size gifts, and many made small gifts.

And although we ended up with 60 gifts of a thousand dollars, more than half of the $1 million goal came from just 10 large gifts.

STEP 4

Pause for a Reality Check

I've suggested you dream big and set bold, breathtaking goals. But before you begin asking for money, you need to know whether the largest gifts you'll be seeking are realistic. That means knowing there are individuals within your organization's reach who have enough money *and* sufficient interest to consider making the largest gifts on your fundraising chart.

Without that information, you're flying blind.

■ How do you know what's real?

Begin by taking a good look at the Table of Gifts you've drawn up. Make a list of the top 10 gifts you'll need.

Now make a second list of the people most likely

to contribute large gifts. To qualify, it's not enough that they have money. You must also have a sense of *why* they might be interested in your project and some point of contact with them. Unless you live in Seattle and know him, don't waste your time on the hope that Bill Gates will donate to your local community center.

The final task is to match the names of potential donors to the actual gifts they might make. Your combined list might look something like this:

HOW MANY NEEDED	GIFT SIZE	PROSPECTIVE DONORS
1	$250,000	Jean Moravia Sam Landry
2	$100,000	Ellen Norton Carol Galler Grayson Miller Alton Fdn.
4	$50,000	Linda Kramer Lawrence Fdn. J.F. Livingston
8	$25,000	Steven Camper Halbrook Corp. Kenny Gascon Jeremy Lavin

At this stage, you don't have to identify *all* of your prospective donors, but you should be able to pinpoint many of them. As in the illustration above, you may only have three people in mind for $50,000 gifts, though you need four. And perhaps you've only identified four who could give $25,000. This isn't necessarily a problem; it just shows you have work to do.

■ The role of consultants

Now it's time to do a field test.

To determine if your goals are realistic, you need to contact the people who might reasonably be expected to make a large gift. Your goal is to learn whether they'd consider a gift in the range you have in mind for them.

But who should approach these individuals, you or a consultant? A layperson or a professional? Okay, let me do my best to be objective.

If you look in the back of this book, the About the Author section in particular, you'll see I'm a consultant and have been for nearly 30 years. So it won't surprise you to hear me tout the advantages of a professional. But, alas, we don't come cheap. Many organizations can't afford our services and, I should add, plenty have tackled campaigns on their own.

Take Jeanne as an example. When she and her board set about raising $600,000 for an environmental project, she dove right in. She bought a good book on fundraising and read it every night. With the help of the book, she developed her table of gifts and made a list of everyone she knew, or could think of, who might have interest in her project. The list totaled some 60 people and Jeanne prioritized them according to how much she thought they could give.

Then, with enviable determination, she set about getting to know and involving the top 10 people on her list. And, because she was also busy planning her project, at every opportunity she'd invite some of her prospects to help with the plans.

Were Jeanne and her board successful? They're still getting to know their donors and haven't yet approached them for money, but I suspect they will be.

It may take them a bit longer than if they'd hired a consultant. But Jeanne's unflagging energy and determination, combined with her small but committed board of volunteers, are likely to carry them across the finish line.

But if, unlike Jeanne, you decide to hire a consultant, his or her role in the early stages of your campaign is pivotal. Your consultant will discuss your project with your best prospects. He or she will uncover what prospective donors think of your organization, and whether this particular project inspires enough excitement to generate the gifts you'll need. A consultant will also evaluate your competition, and identify the other factors (a competing campaign, for instance) that may affect your ability to succeed. While consultants won't actually ask people for gifts, they can help you determine each donor's giving potential.

Once your consultant has spoken with a sufficient number of people (usually 20 to 30 for a local project), he or she will be able to tell you with some degree of objectivity whether you should proceed and how much you can likely raise.

Now, you might think consultants will *always* recommend your going forward – they want to continue drawing a paycheck, after all. But, remember, reputations, recommendations, and future business are on the line here. If a consultant thinks you're unlikely to succeed, he or she will almost always tell you so. And while they can't guarantee success, consultants will also let you know whether your project has a real chance of succeeding.

If it does, then you're ready to go to the next step. If it doesn't, you've still got work to do.

■ How one last interview changed the whole game

Sometimes the organized process of talking with

community leaders and potential large donors yields surprising results.

A few years ago, I worked with a hospice in central New York to help them determine if they had a chance of raising money for a new building. We spent several hours developing and reviewing a list of 40 people we should interview. The list included board members, donors, public officials, and a few who were major donors to other community organizations, though not big givers to the hospice.

After 27 interviews, the prospect for raising much money looked pretty dim. Many were interested, but no one indicated they'd consider making the top gift.

I was about to recommend the hospice either delay or scale back its project – a result no one would have liked. But before finalizing my recommendation, I decided, one more time, to try scheduling an interview with a promising prospect who had thus far put me off.

Michael, a businessman in the area, had a passing relationship with the hospice, but it wasn't particularly strong. In fact, he and his wife were major donors to a competitor organization. He hadn't responded to my previous requests for an interview, but much to my surprise, when I called a seventh time, Michael agreed to see me. The meeting was most fortuitous!

It turned out Michael owned a building he'd been trying to sell that was in the right location and was the right size for my client. In our meeting, Michael told me he'd consider *giving* the building to the hospice, getting a costly liability off his balance sheet and taking advantage of a charitable deduction to boot.

The building was worth $750,000, and eventually it became the lead gift we needed to anchor the campaign. Of course, as with most projects, the road wasn't entirely smooth. Some board members weren't sure they liked the building. Then there was the issue that the facility was about a third larger than they needed, adding that much more maintenance expense. Yes, the hospice did, as the old saying goes, "look a gift horse in the mouth."

But after a host of meetings, some of which were heated, the hospice decided to accept Michael's building. And with that gift, a successful project began to seem inevitable. That tail-end interview made all the difference.

Michael's gift of the building highlights once again the importance of testing your project in the community with the people who can make a difference.

STEP 5

Identify and Enlist a Campaign Chair

One of the most important decisions you'll make is the selection of a Campaign Chair. That's the person whose role it is to stand up in public, sound the fundraising call, and inspire others to follow.

It takes steely courage, dogged resolve, and generous passion (along with a healthy dose of blind faith) to be the public face of a high stakes venture. And raising $1 million *is* a high stakes venture. While your Chair will get kudos if the fundraising succeeds, he or she risks looking like a failure if the venture falls short.

I've known organizations that have taken literally a year to fill the post – that's how daunting the job can be.

When Planned Parenthood in Philadelphia was

planning its campaign, the board spent half a dozen meetings trying to identify just the right chair. Ten years earlier the affiliate had completed a successful campaign and the leaders who had worked on that effort were still engaged but no longer willing to take the lead. They thought, rightly, that it was time for the next generation to step up. But as is often the case, the next generation's leaders weren't as seasoned or as well-known as their predecessors.

As fate would have it, the right person was just under their noses. Kim, a member of the board, had the passion, energy, and time to make a good chair though she'd never served in that capacity. When the board chair asked Kim if she'd be willing, she agreed as long as she could find a co-chair to work with her.

Kim tapped her friend Sara. While she didn't have a long history with Planned Parenthood, she was passionate about women's issues and, like Kim, had personal wealth to bring to the campaign. But even more important was the high quality commitment they brought to the project. Month after month, meeting after meeting, they worked until every last dollar was raised.

Michael, the individual I mentioned earlier who donated the hospice building, provides another interesting campaign chair story. Once he decided to give the building, Michael wanted to be sure the campaign to renovate it was successful. He knew that a plaque bearing his name would grace the building.

In a conversation with the board chair, Michael let on that he might be willing to chair the campaign. He was a powerful man in the community. And he was quite sure if he chaired the campaign and made a handful of calls, he could help ensure its success.

So, despite the fact that Michael didn't have a longstanding or strong relationship with the organization, he chaired the campaign. And, yes, very successfully. The resulting building was everything he and the hospice board hoped it would be.

As was the case here, it's not uncommon for small organizations to enlist an outsider. Often, these small groups don't have the kind of day-to-day connections with people of influence and affluence in their communities. And while it's often the case that these individuals aren't interested in serving on your board or coming to meeting after meeting, they may be willing to help you reach the next level by chairing or co-chairing a campaign.

■ The job of campaign chair

Of all the jobs in fundraising, being a campaign chair is both the most frustrating and most exhilarating.

Frustrating because it falls to the chair to be dogged when others come up short. Exhilarating because there's nothing quite like having someone tell you he'll contribute a large gift to your project.

Let's look at the chair's actual duties:

First, he or she will make a personally significant gift. In many cases, the chair's gift will be one of the largest. But in some cases a truly generous smaller gift that represents a stretch will suffice.

Second, the chair will play an important role in soliciting gifts – the largest gifts. And, yes, while this is a challenge, many of the campaign chairs I've worked with have warmed to the task because of the generosity they've encountered.

Third, your chair will help to shape the campaign. Exactly how will depend on the strengths of the specific person, but a campaign chair often works side-by-side with the executive director and development director, with each complementing and supporting the others. When this arrangement works, it's like a good marriage: gradually, your chair and the campaign team learn to trust one another and build on each others' strengths.

Fourth, your chair is the public face of the campaign, lending his or her name to the project and letting the organization piggyback on his or her credibility in the community. You can imagine just how risky this is if there isn't strong assurance the campaign will succeed.

Finally, your campaign chair has a grab bag of other duties. He or she runs committee meetings, encourages the staff and other board members, talks to the press when needed, helps celebrate milestones (large and small), and thanks the people who make success possible.

As you can surmise, the job takes a special kind of person! And from my experience of working with dozens of campaign chairs, I believe that to do the job well a chair needs three specific traits:

- A passion for the cause
- Personal generosity
- Follow-through; the ability of the person to do what she says she's going to do

And with apologies to the 70s rock group, Meatloaf, I learned when working with Morris that two out of three *is* bad.

A retired college president, Morris had sway in his community. He knew lots of people and had time on his hands. And for years he had known Larry, the director of the child center. So Morris seemed an obvious choice to chair the campaign. Without much consideration, Larry tapped him for the role, starting the campaign on an excruciating path.

While Morris really did know everyone and everyone knew Morris, and most people even liked him, the ex-president didn't follow through when it came to asking for money. He just couldn't muster the courage to sit down and ask someone face-to-face.

Again and again, Larry had to pick up the pieces. Morris would write a letter to a major donor asking for the gift, but he wouldn't make the all-important follow-up call. Or, rather than scheduling a meeting to ask for a gift, he would mention the campaign casually at a cocktail party where he happened to run into a donor he was supposed to solicit. And once again, he wouldn't follow up.

To make matters worse, once Morris was ensconced as campaign chair, he wasn't about to relinquish the post. He liked chairing the committee meetings. He loved taking credit for all of Larry's fundraising successes. And he liked feeling important – the way he had when he was a college president!

What might have been a smooth-sailing campaign became an immense burden for Larry. He had to do his own work *and* cover for Morris.

So even though Morris had passion for the cause, and he and his wife made a generous personal gift, he lacked the third and perhaps most important quality – the courage and will and determination to follow through.

Fortunately, it's easy to find out in advance whether people like Morris are likely to be good campaign chairs, because of...

Campaign Rule
People are consistent.

Those of us who struggle with our own foibles know how hard it is to change. More often than not, our basic patterns of behavior have a way of recurring despite our best efforts.

This may be a curse when you're struggling to stop smoking or resist sweets, but it's a blessing when you look at your strengths. And it's a great help when you're choosing a campaign chair.

Why? Because the same consistent tendencies we see in ourselves allow us to spot predictive patterns in others.

Take the case of Rose, the astute director of a community center in Pennsylvania. Rose was planning a campaign to raise $1 million to renovate the main program space.

Rose's board members encouraged her to consider Bill for the campaign chair. He served on the board and had been active in developing the fundraising plans. Bill was also powerful in the community, heading up a good-sized foundation. He liked to be "in the know" and was often asked to participate in community projects. Time after time, Bill would show up at meetings and dominate the discussion. On the surface, he seemed like the perfect choice to bring stature and skill to the Center's campaign, not to mention a healthy gift from his foundation.

But as Rose watched Bill closely, she saw something that troubled her. When the time came for taking on assignments, he seldom volunteered. And when he did offer to help, he usually didn't follow through. Rose reluctantly concluded that, although Bill liked to be a big shot, he didn't like doing the work.

Surmising all of this made it possible for Rose to convince her board chair to by-pass Bill as campaign chair. Had she chosen him, his habitual behaviors would likely have undermined the campaign. And the chances he would have risen to the occasion on this one project, when he had failed to on so many others, were slim to none.

Thanks to Rose's perceptiveness and her belief that people are consistent, Bill stayed a committee member, where he didn't do much good, but at least he didn't do much harm. And yes, Bill's foundation did give $150,000 anyway.

■ Two Campaign Chairs who really dug in

Let me share two stories about how good Chairs helped two very different campaigns succeed:

• CAROL G.

Carol G. was an unlikely choice. She'd never done much fundraising, and certainly had never chaired a campaign.

She had been asked to serve on the board of her local Planned Parenthood, in part because the organization's board and fundraising committee needed to reach into the younger generation of donors and Carol G. was a well-respected member of that demographic.

When Carol G. joined the board, she felt like an outsider. Most of the volunteers were in their 60s and 70s and, as in many communities, these older board members had developed strong bonds over many years. So Carol G. was surprised when the Board Chair asked her to co-chair the campaign alongside Sam, an older, well-established board member.

Carol G. was reluctant at first, but because she was passionate about the cause and realized it was a chance to learn new skills, she finally said yes.

Carol G.'s tenure didn't get off to a strong start. In

the beginning, she regularly deferred to her more experienced colleague. But gradually, as she developed her fundraising and leadership skills, she moved from feeling like an outsider to leading the campaign with spirit, energy, and humor.

And as she grew more comfortable, she began to tap into the energy and generosity of her generation of donors, just as the board chair had hoped. Carol G. played a major role in all aspects of the campaign, working well with the Executive Director, the Development Director and Sam, her Campaign Co-chair.

By the end of the campaign, Carol G. no longer felt like a fundraising novice. She made her largest gift ever to the drive. She ran meetings with ease. She solicited gifts like a veteran.

How did she go from novice to "campaign pro"?

Carol G. was able to grow into her role because, like every good Campaign Chair, she had passion for the cause, was generous, and followed through. Equally important to Carol G.'s success was her wonderful sense of humor. In meeting after meeting, she was able to turn frustrating setbacks into tales of comedy.

• **CAROLE H.**

When the Arden Theatre of Philadelphia decided to build a new performance space, Carole H. was asked to chair the campaign. Carole's husband, Otto, had died some years before and the new theatre was to be named in his honor.

Carole is a quiet woman with a heart as big as a bus, often honored for her remarkable generosity, and who *does what she says she'll do*. She's got the passion, generosity, and follow-through any campaign leader should have. And just by being who she is, she infuses them into every project she takes on.

As was her way, Carole played a huge role in making the Arden Theater's campaign a success. She solicited many people. She lent her name. She was a cheerleader, and led by example with an early, generous gift. And, the soul of grace, she passed all the glory and recognition on to her late husband.

The Arden's staff was so appreciative they found an appropriate way to thank Carole. One morning, when the campaign was over and the dust had settled, they led her upstairs to the room where props are stored. They pulled a white sheet off of a large piece of granite. There in the granite were inscribed the words, "Carole H., the real cornerstone of our campaign."

In that quiet and unceremonial fashion, they told her they wanted to install the piece of granite in the corner of the building – a literal cornerstone – to honor what she had done.

What I recall from that moment was Carole's long pause. She had worked so hard to honor the life and memory of her late husband, that the shift of attention to her was overwhelming.

Now, many years later, the cornerstone serves as a reminder of this wonderful woman's steady, understated qualities – the qualities we look for in every campaign chair.

■ It's worth the search

If you're in a hurry and you question the prudence of finding just the right chair, even if it means delaying your campaign, remember this:

A poor chair will drag you down.

An "okay" chair will keep you afloat.

But a *great* fundraising chair will give your campaign wings!

STEP 6

Build a Committee

When Steve and Elizabeth, the founders of a small theatre company grew frustrated with committees and decided they could do it themselves, they were right!

Steve and Elizabeth set about renovating a small performance space in their town. They went through the motions of building a committee, but Steve and Elizabeth thought – in fact, they knew – they could do everything more effectively and quickly by themselves. After all, who knew more about the organization than they did?

The only problem was that when they were done, no one else had a feeling of ownership in the project and the very people Steve and Elizabeth needed to help grow their audience felt distant and unconnected. Without board members and volunteers advocating for the theatre – drawing in their families and friends and colleagues – attendance languished. In fact, within two years Steve and Elizabeth closed shop. They felt their immense effort wasn't appreciated and they moved to another city where they hoped for more.

The lesson? Fundraising isn't only about raising money, it's also about involving people in a project through their time, energy, *and* money. And campaign committees are one of the best ways to do that.

So, yes, in addition to a chair, you need a committee. It may seem tempting to do it all yourself. And it's true committees *do* gobble up time. But a well-run fundraising committee serves three important functions:

• It offers a way to involve people, which will make them even more generous donors

• It increases gifts by multiplying the number of connections between the campaign and prospective donors, and

• It adds capacity to get the solicitations done.

■ Friends asking friends

While you personally may be the best fundraiser in the world, you'll still increase the chances of securing generous gifts from a wide range of people if they're asked to contribute *by someone they know.*

When a friend who's already contributed asks you for a gift, it's darn hard to refuse. And a committee of volunteers provides a powerful network of people who can approach their friends.

It's true that many resist asking their friends. Again and again, you hear volunteers say, "I'll ask for money, but I won't go to my friends." And that's understandable – people are concerned about potentially damaging their friendships. But friends asking friends is a key ingredient in fundraising, and part of *your* job is to help volunteers and committee members overcome their hesitation.

I understand personally how difficult this can be! Several years ago, my younger daughter Carla was involved in what I felt was a groundbreaking theater project. As one of the lead performers (Carla plays the violin), she not only developed the show, but also had to raise a good deal of money for it. And, no fool she, Carla came to me for assistance. When I set out to help her troupe, I found that I too had to overcome my worries about approaching friends.

What a shock! I'd spent years teaching campaign leaders how to coax people over this hurdle, and here I was stuck on it in a big way. In fact, I was so concerned about asking friends that it was hard to determine whom I might approach.

Fortunately, I found a way to talk myself into asking. I realized this would be a prime opportunity to test *and* practice what I preach to clients, and that got me fired up to try.

I started by making a generous gift from my own pocket, to be sure I was fully committed. (There's nothing like writing a check to test your commitment! Talk is easy, writing a check isn't.)

Campaign Rule
We must give before we can ask others

I then made a list of all of my friends who I believed had resources and were fans of my daughter or her music. One by one – starting with those I was most comfortable with – I went and asked each for a specific gift according to their perceived means. I made sure to only ask people who I thought would enjoy being part of my daughter's support group.

I must confess that when I approached my closest friend, I had to swallow hard. I worried I was putting her in a position where she couldn't say no. Maybe she'd resent me and it would harm our friendship. I mustered the courage anyway, and though the moment felt awkward for both of us, she was genuinely happy to support Carla's project. (Had she said no, I admit it would have been delicate. But I think we would have talked it through enough to get past our shared discomfort.)

There were many friends I didn't ask! I knew some would have zero interest in Carla's avant garde ventures. I didn't want them to give simply because of me, but because they enjoyed supporting a remarkable artist who happens to be my daughter.

While it's a fundraising truism that we shouldn't make up other people's minds for them, it's also true we should approach people who are likely to have some interest in the project rather than approaching people just because they have money!

In the end, and much to my delight, just about everyone I asked gave, and gave generously. And those who didn't respond, well, that was fine too. Many who gave even flew to Chicago to see the premiere of Carla's new piece, and were excited to be part of her "production team."

After it was all over, one of my friends who had given generously told me that supporting Carla's work reminded him of when he was young and did things out of creative passion. He actually thanked me several times over the next few months for helping him reconnect with his own creative spirit.

The key point I'm making with Carla's story is this: Had I asked people who weren't friends or who had no interest in the project, the chances of their making a gift would have been remote at best. And the same thing is true for your organization. *Although it's a challenge, when friends ask friends, they usually achieve excellent results.*

■ More involvement means more giving

While the value of a campaign committee starts with friends asking friends, it doesn't stop there. A second important benefit is *involvement.*

Campaign Rule
With involvement comes investment

As we've already noted, most people will give when asked by friends. But, we give more when friends ask on behalf of an organization we're already involved with or for a cause we're known to favor. Think of it this way. When faced with these three scenarios, which one would prompt you to give *more?*

• A friend asks you for a donation for her favorite cause

• Someone you don't know very well asks you to give to your favorite cause

• A friend asks you to join her in making a gift to an organization you're both deeply involved with

I'll bet you chose the third. Most people make their most generous gifts when friends ask them to contribute to an organization in which they have a direct and immediate involvement. And working on the fundraising committee is one of the most direct and immediate types of involvement organizations can offer.

I think of my friend Sol, who for much of his adult life has been troubled by the issue of homelessness. For Sol, who comes from an immigrant family, the idea of not having a home is horrifying and he identifies deeply with people in that condition. Over the years, Sol has given money to the homeless shelters in his community. He gives quietly, without fanfare, and often anonymously. In fact, only his closest friends know of his passion for and support of this issue.

Is it any wonder that when one of Sol's good friends, who serves on the board of a shelter, asked him for a sizable gift Sol was pleased to be asked and eager to make a gift? Of course not! Sol's friend had merely done him a good turn by offering him a way to help eradicate homelessness in his own community.

If you remember that nonprofits are simply the vehicles through which we each can make a difference in the world, the asking becomes much easier, especially when the organization's mission happens to match our own passions.

■ Committees create "bench strength"

The third benefit of having a committee, beyond engaging people and establishing a broader network of friends, is that it adds to your ranks.

It takes a lot of people to solicit gifts. The Table of Gifts I shared with you earlier showed that, while the bulk of your money will come from 10 gifts, the remainder will come from *many* donors. And for every gift you hope to secure (particularly as you go down the chart), you'll usually have to ask not one but two or three or even four people.

If, for example, you're looking for 20 gifts of $5,000 each, it's likely to take 50 or even 60 solicitations to reach that goal. That's far too many for one person (or even two or three people) to accomplish. To solicit that many people, you'll need a dozen effective volunteers.

■ Taking the bold approach

Hudson Guild is a Settlement House on New York's west side, with a mission focused on building a strong and vibrant community. When the Guild began its most recent fundraising campaign, Brian, who was primarily responsible for fundraising, decided to recruit a campaign committee made up of some of the organization's largest donors. The goal was to involve them more fully in the Guild's fundraising planning.

But it felt like a risky move. What if some of these big donors agreed to join the committee and the committee meetings were a bust? Or what if these powerful people came together as a campaign committee and started pushing to make changes the staff didn't want?

These were good reasons for anxiety, but none outweighed the advantages of having a truly powerhouse committee.

So, Brian, with the approval of his executive director, approached his campaign chair and asked him to concentrate on recruiting some of the Guild's top contributors. They began with a former board member (her gift later sparked the entire campaign), before moving on to the most powerful Guild supporter of all.

The campaign chair picked up the phone and called Peter. Like many powerful people, he has strong opinions and before agreeing to get involved he peppered the chair with some tough questions. "How do you know this project can succeed?" "Shouldn't you spend money on your programs rather than building renovations?" "Who else will be on the committee?" "How many meetings will I have to come to?"

The campaign chair answered these and many more questions. He also brought in the executive director to address additional concerns. It was like a prosecutor grilling a defendant. But eventually Peter was satisfied and agreed to serve on the campaign committee.

From there it got easier. Peter was eager for his daughter to learn about nonprofits and encouraged her to join the team too. Then, once Peter and his daughter were on board, a local foundation head signed on, as did another former board member with considerable clout.

Despite all of Brian's earlier anxieties, the committee worked wonders. Under them, the campaign goal increased substantially and each committee member gave generously to help reach the new goal. Many of the members also opened doors to other donors whom the Guild couldn't have reached without them.

While there are precious few things in fundraising I feel unequivocal about, this is one of them: If you're serious about raising $1 million, do *not* attempt it in isolation. There's far too much opportunity value inherent in a committee to take the seemingly easier, do-it-yourself route.

■ **Who should be on the committee?**

In general, you're looking for *three* types of people to serve on your campaign committee:

• Those who can make the largest gifts (as in the Hudson Guild example). Often, these individuals are also the best solicitors;

• People who are wonderful workers and are passionate about the project though they might not be well-off; and, finally,

• People whose presence will broaden your reach – connected individuals who are interested but not yet engaged with you.

Surprisingly, people in the first group may be the easiest to find. That's because, in the process of implementing STEPS 1 through 5, you've already identified potential major donors. In fact, you or your consultant have likely spoken with them already. These potential committee members already know about your project and you know their level of interest.

■ **How should you approach potential committee members?**

Jeanne, founder of an organization working to protect the waterfront environment of a poor urban area of New York City, was preparing to ask people to serve on her campaign committee. (Jeanne is the woman I mentioned earlier who decided to forego the use of a consultant).

The Alliance had been developing plans to renovate an old firehouse to serve as a center for environmental justice and education in the heart of the community.

Jeanne's board was passionate about the project but most of their members weren't able to make a large gift. If they hoped to raise $1 million, the board had to recruit other well-to-do people.

Jeanne developed a list of candidates, but she had only second or third-hand connections with most of them. And, frankly, no matter how persuasive Jeanne was about the project, it was unlikely any would return her phone call, much less join her campaign committee.

But one new board member, Deborah, was able to open a door that led to successfully recruiting a strong campaign committee. While Deborah herself wasn't a power-player, her father was. He lived in the area and was interested in both the environment and education. And as Deborah became more engaged in the project, she shared with him the assorted materials Jeanne developed for the board.

The project sparked his interest and he asked to come to a board meeting to get a sense of its members and how they operated. He was warmly welcomed and Jeanne smartly used that meeting to present the basics of the campaign plan, including the project description, gift chart, and proposed timetable.

After the meeting, Jeanne scheduled a meeting with Deborah and her dad to discuss how they might help. She asked if they'd consider:

- Co-chairing the campaign.
- Making the lead gift.
- Helping to identify and recruit two or three other power players in the community.

Jeanne knew if they'd agree to these three things, the campaign would be up and running. A lead gift and powerful name committed early in the process would establish the credibility Jeanne needed to get others on board. For Deborah and her father, it was actually quite easy. They liked the project. They had confidence in Jeanne, and they were happy to have something to work on together.

With Deborah and her father on board, the next committee recruits came not from Jeanne's long-shot list of wealthy people, but from select individuals Deborah and her father knew well and could more easily approach.

Jeanne's story may seem like an unusual fairy tale – one person, one family unlocking the way to success.

But in fact recruiting one or two powerful people early in the campaign is the way major gifts fundraising usually works. It requires patience and doggedness. But identifying and recruiting the right group is absolutely essential to your success.

As I write this, Deborah and her father and friends are just becoming engaged. It looks promising so far, but Jeanne has a long way to go. My instincts, however, tell me they'll be able to create a successful campaign.

■ What the committee does

Your fundraising committee provides a sounding board for many of the decisions that shape the fundraising process. Early on, the committee will review critical questions such as: Is the goal right? Are the objectives too broad or too narrow? Is the fundraising budget adequate? Is the proposed timetable reasonable?

Then, once the plan is in place, the committee shifts to monitoring and course correction as needed. They'll review questions like: Are we on track to reach the goal? Are we on budget for the fundraising? What's our plan to raise the rest of the money?

But the committee is more than a sounding board or monitor. It also works on other specific aspects of the campaign. How will donors be acknowledged? Will there be opportunities for naming programs and buildings? Over how many years can a donor pay off his or her pledge?

Oh yes, and there's another key responsibility. Every committee member is expected to make a generous gift, one that pushes the boundaries of their personal giving limit. For some, this might be a relatively small, but stretch amount, while others are likely to make gifts at the top of the gift table.

If this surprises you, you're not alone. I remember Ed, who agreed to serve on the committee for a small campaign for a community housing project. A retired businessman, Ed agreed to solicit other businesses.

When the chair asked him for a generous personal gift, Ed was taken aback. For years Ed donated money from the company he worked for. Now that he was retired, it was his own money he had to part with. And for all of his generosity, he found it hard to do (though he did give a small gift in the end).

The final responsibility of those serving on your fundraising committee is to solicit gifts from within their own networks. Some members may develop a team of their own to accomplish this.

In the $1.1 million campaign for Lancaster's Community Market, Kathy was such a committee member. For years, she has done her grocery shopping at the Market – a bustling place dense with food stands and produce. She was passionate about the experience.

So the Market's Campaign Director invited Kathy to join the committee *and* to assemble a group of other likeminded shoppers to help with soliciting.

Initially, Kathy was hesitant. She didn't like fundraising and hadn't ever asked people for money. But she loved the market, so somewhat reluctantly, she signed on.

The eight other shoppers Kathy recruited were mostly friends – people she ran into on Tuesday and Friday mornings when they were all at the Market.

Kathy and her Market friends formed a team that mustered the will and the courage to ask other shoppers for money. It wasn't easy for them. In fact, it took several meetings before the group settled in to the fundraising mode and some opted out when they realized they'd actually have to ask their friends for a gift. But once the group got to work, they did a great job of identifying other shoppers, evaluating what they thought they might give, and asking for the gifts.

Ultimately this small group of Market shoppers raised over $100,000. Each of them made generous gifts themselves and became surprisingly fearless at asking others.

STEP 7

Ask for the Largest Gifts First

Remember Art, the Community Market board member who was convinced the group could raise a half a million dollars from 500 gifts of $1000 each?

Art's belief that raising money through lots of smaller gifts isn't uncommon. And certainly you'll want to invite as many people as possible to contribute what they can. But *before* you approach smaller donors you need enough large gifts to anchor the campaign. You ignore this part of the fundraising process at your own peril!

Take the temptation of direct mail, for instance. Blanketing your community with a general appeal is certainly easier than summoning the courage to ask selected people for sizable gifts. Just ask the Manheim Township Library, where a wonderful group of people decided they were going to raise $2.2 million from private sources to help expand the library. They did in fact raise $900,000 in major gifts, leaving them $1.3 million short.

Approximately 34,000 people live in Manheim and their small trailer-like library was very popular. So the board figured they could send a letter to everyone asking for help to build a new facility. They wrote a great letter, developed a pledge form, and secured all of the town's names and addresses. They even put personal notes on many of the letters. With great anticipation, the letter was sent.

How much of the hoped-for $1.2 million came in from that mailing? To the board's surprise, just over $14,000. Not nearly enough to complete the campaign.

With some rare exceptions, the direct mail approach results in small gifts. To succeed in raising the remaining $1.2 million, the Manheim Library needs additional big gifts. Who do you know would send $10,000, $25,000 and $50,000 via the post?

Raising large gifts requires effort, but it's a more strategic kind of effort, not the many hours of volunteer work required to get out a mailing. It takes time and thought and energy to build solid relationships with the right people, but once that's done, the asking part is easy.

Let me again cite Jim, the founder of the Science Factory. Over the course of two years, Jim got to know many in his community who were interested in science. In particular, Jim befriended Harold.

Harold was retired and lived quietly. When he was a young man, he invented a piece of aircraft equipment that eventually made him wealthy. But Harold kept a low profile in the community. He lived in a modest house and had none of the usual trappings of wealth. In fact, the only reason Jim had any inkling of Harold's resources was through a mutual friend.

As Jim came to know Harold, he learned that his new friend had grown up tinkering with all sorts of things in his basement workshop. He had become an inventor, not because of his schooling, but because he liked to tear things apart and rebuild them.

Early in their relationship, Jim asked Harold for a donation and received a relatively modest gift of $5,000. Jim kept involving him in one aspect and another of the project planning. One day, Harold called Jim and said, "I've been thinking about the workshop you're building in the Science Factory. We'd like to give you $50,000 for that. It's the kind of place I got my start, tinkering around. Maybe it'll have the same effect on someone else."

While that's a substantial gift and a good story, the

real power of this friendship and mutual interest may well play out in even bigger ways in the years to come. It wouldn't surprise me if Harold goes on to increase his giving five or ten times over. Genuine relationships with donors build over time and result in ongoing, and often dramatic, support.

But what if, like the Manheim Library approach, Harold had simply received a letter in the mail asking for a contribution? Likely he would have given, but nowhere close to $50,000 or even $5,000. The lesson here is that it's critical to take the time and energy to identify people in your community who, along with resources, have some personal reason to be interested in and perhaps even passionate about your project. This intersection of shared interests is what prompts us to be truly generous.

■ Everyone's fundraising fantasy

Rich, the executive director of a youth services organization in New York City established a charter school to expand and extend the services his agency provided for young people and their families in a notably poor neighborhood.

In the first year, the kindergarten and first grades were up and running in classrooms rented to them by a local public school. But wanting to expand, Rich set about planning to build a facility that would accommodate grades K-6.

What Rich wanted was not just a school, but a combination community center and school. He wanted a place where parents could get involved. A place that had theatre and music and sports along with child care and even a health clinic.

For the most part, the board was supportive, but some members had serious concerns. They wondered how Rich could maintain basic operations while devoting significant amounts of time and money to this new goal. And Rich knew that many board members weren't eager to commit their funds while the economy was so gloomy.

But Rich felt they couldn't sit back and wait. He already had waiting lists for the kindergarten class in the fall. The first graders would soon be ready for second grade, and next year he'd need classrooms for the third graders.

In meeting after meeting, Pete, one of the newer board members, sat quietly and attentively, listening and asking questions. He'd been involved as a volunteer for some years and knew firsthand the challenges young people in the community faced. His quiet and thoughtful ways had already earned him respect among the others at the table, but no one anticipated the way he would act on his commitment.

One day, after a particularly challenging meeting, Pete showed up unexpectedly at Rich's office. Fearing the worst, Rich asked his assistant to hold his calls.

Pete began the conversation in his characteristically understated way, telling Rich how important the organization was to him. He predicted dire financial times ahead, but still felt they should move ahead with his plans for a new building.

"This isn't the time to stop growing," Pete said. "This downturn offers opportunities that'll disappear when conditions improve. Land is cheaper, and architects and builders are hungry for work. This is the time to move ahead, not stop and wait."

Then he added, "I know you'll have to invest to get the plans shovel-ready, so I've decided to cover those costs."

And with that he handed Rich a check for $1 million!

Pete's extraordinary gift did much more than provide the planning funds. It created a sense of credibility and inevitability for the project. Board members who had been skeptical stopped their carping. They knew that when the project took clear form – with a site, a plan, and a budget – they'd be asked to give. And because Pete set the standard, they'd be more likely to stretch.

To be sure, Pete's gift was a surprise, but it didn't come out of nowhere. He had been intimately involved with the organization for many years. He had served as a volunteer in the programs, working with a group of young people from the time they were eight until they went on to college. Pete had also attended early planning meetings for the project.

My point is, if you've involved people who are capable of making large gifts in the early steps of your fundraising, you'll be ready to ask them for their commitments without much fuss. One of the counter-intuitive aspects of well-executed fundraising is that the largest gifts are often the easiest to ask for. You won't need fancy proposals or glossy brochures. But unlike Rich, in most cases you will need to *ask*.

■ You're not the only one who's anxious

Dayle, the executive director of a Planned Parenthood affiliate was ready to get the campaign ball rolling. The plans to renovate the clinic and update the entire communications system were in place. Co-chairs were on board. And the committee was taking shape.

Now it was time to think about a leadership gift.

Dayle knew that one of the co-chairs, Kim,

intended to make a gift. But she didn't know how large and she wasn't sure she was the right person to ask. The days dragged on and, because the gift would hopefully set the standard for the campaign, the situation nagged at Dayle.

Not wanting to delay any more, she picked up the phone and called, explaining to Kim why she wanted to meet. "Great. I've been anxious about this too," said the co-chair.

When they met over lunch, Dayle brought along the gift chart and nothing else. Following some pleasantries and an appetizer, she pulled the chart from her purse, keeping her cool all the while. Looking at it together, she and Kim found the right gift amount – one that was clearly a leadership gift and also suited Kim's giving capacity.

They parted with a sense of mutual relief. Kim not only had agreed to a substantial gift, but having made her own commitment she now felt she could muster the courage to solicit her co-chair for a gift that matched her own – which in fact is what happened.

Campaign Rule
We must give before we can ask others

After making their own gifts, it was much easier for these co-chairs to approach the rest of the committee as well as several key prospective donors. Soon, they tied down well over half of the goal just by soliciting people who were already involved.

The campaign built a head of steam and a collective confidence that enabled them to reach out to others, both within the Planned Parenthood community and beyond.

■ It's stressful but critical

Securing these early (large) gifts often creates more anxiety than any other part of the campaign. So much depends on them! You simply can't make up for a lack of big gifts by raising many smaller ones. And, just as importantly, you won't have established the sense of inevitability that encourages others to give.

Often major donors who have been involved from the start will be ready to make their commitments early. But if they're not, you'll have to bring them along and help them understand the importance of early leadership giving.

Jay, the executive director of a hospital foundation, knew he'd have to do that with Marvin, who hadn't been involved in any of the early planning of the new Breast Care Center.

Jay knew his project might interest Marvin, whose wife had died of breast cancer. But rather than ask him at the outset for a large gift, Jay took great care to engage Marvin more fully. He showed him the plan, invited him to meet with the oncologist who was developing the program, and introduced him to some of the campaign committee members.

As Marvin become more engaged, he began wondering whether he could name the facility in honor of his wife. And when he asked about the possibility, Jay was ready with a table of gifts and a donor recognition plan that outlined the various naming opportunities.

And what happened? Of course you know. Marvin gave $1.5 million and the Breast Care Center was named in his wife's honor. Jay's patient approach was highly stressful but in the end well worth it, as Marvin's gift proved critical to the success of the entire campaign.

STEP 8

Ask the Insiders Next

Some time ago, I worked on a campaign for a public library. With some fits and starts, Renee, the campaign chair, and Mary, the library director, had successfully tied down most of the large gifts.

Now they were ready to solicit those who weren't large donors but who were close to the library. These included staff members, volunteers, and a host of people who used the library almost daily.

But as Renee and Mary pored over the list of staff members, they grew increasingly anxious. The library's public funding, like that of libraries throughout the state, had been cut and cut again; and staff members hadn't received a raise for some time. Earlier that year, Mary even had to eliminate a position.

"Should we really ask staff members for money?"

asked Renee. "I'm afraid they'll throw eggs at me."

Mary was uncomfortable, too. She knew some of the staff loved the place but others were so frustrated by the lack of resources and flat salaries that they were on the verge of leaving.

Mary and Renee had all but decided to forego asking staff to support ... until Jerry intervened.

Jerry, who had worked at the library for probably a decade and never missed a day, was a developmentally delayed adult who lived with his parents. He cleaned the restrooms, mopped the floors, emptied the trash, and performed a host of other custodial functions. Many who frequented the library knew and loved Jerry; he was always friendly and helpful. But because his salary was so low, he was one of the people Mary and Renee couldn't imagine asking for a gift.

So when Jerry walked into the office carrying a check for one thousand dollars made out to the library, Mary nearly teetered from her chair.

"What's this, Jerry?" she asked.

"I've been hearing people talk about plans to make this building better," he replied, "and I'd like to help. I'm tired of trying to clean these old floors that simply won't look clean no matter what I do. This job is my life and I'd like to help get some floors that'll shine like new. "

That moment was a turning point for Mary and her campaign chair. Jerry taught them not to make assumptions about who would give and who wouldn't. His gift also taught them that people often give for very personal reasons.

When, a few weeks later, Jerry presented his gift to the library board – something he asked to do – tissues dabbed at every eye. And when the library renovation was completed, there was no mistaking Jerry's pride as he made his new floors gleam every day.

It's hard not to be generous when we see people who don't have great resources give extraordinary gifts. I'm sure Jerry's inspired generous gifts from many board and staff members who might have otherwise held back. And it gave Mary and Renee the courage to ask everyone.

■ Who are *your* insiders?

Every organization has a band of insiders. Among these are staff, board members, advisory council, volunteers, people who rely on your services, founders, and former board members. These people, while they may have limited means, are likely to be fond of and perhaps even committed to your cause.

It's time to turn your focus to these insiders once you've established the inevitability of your project by raising most of the large gifts.

Their numbers may be relatively small – perhaps 100. Even so, you'll need approximately 20 volunteers if you hope to solicit all of them. And enlisting this broader group of solicitors may be among your most challenging tasks.

One campaign committee with which I'm familiar developed several working groups to handle the task. Each group was formed to solicit people who shared their characteristics. There was a Next Generation Group made up of people in their 30s and 40s that reached out to other Gen X-ers. There was a second group in their 60's, 70's and 80's who approached other retirees. Lastly, a group of former board members reached out to past trustees.

I suspect you may be thinking, "Hey, these folks are already insiders. They know how important this project is. All they need is a letter from us." That's a fine strategy – but only if you want a handful of token gifts. If you desire thoughtful, larger gifts, you'll still need people talking directly to people!

■ There are many ways to contribute

When Bonnie set out to solicit her hospice staff, she invited a few of the best-liked workers to be part of the process. She and several committee members met with them a number of times to brainstorm the best way to invite *every* staff member to contribute.

One easy way, Bonnie and her team decided, was through payroll deductions. But, more creatively, they encouraged staff members to come up with their own ways of raising money. And some hatched surprising ideas.

Sandy was a nurse at the hospice. The single mother of two kids who were headed for college, she was a short, stocky woman with a friendly smile and a great sense of humor.

When Bonnie asked her to help solicit her fellow staff members, Sandy wasn't sure what to do. *How can I ask others if I can't afford even a small gift?* she wondered.

It took her several days, but Sandy finally hit upon a solution. Over the next couple of weeks, she approached her colleagues and asked if they would sponsor her in doing sit-ups. She set a goal – six weeks away – of doing as many sit-ups as she could, on the floor of the staff kitchen at lunchtime.

Now, Sandy doesn't look like someone who can do many sit-ups, so when she asked fellow staff members for 25 cents per, people figured their liability was limited.

But Sandy had wanted to trim down, and every day

when she got home from work, she did sit-ups. And when she was watching her favorite TV show, she did sit-ups. And every morning before breakfast, she did sit-ups.

You know where this is headed. When the time came for Sandy's demonstration, she shocked everyone in the staff kitchen. She did ten sit-ups. Twenty. Thirty. Fifty. One hundred. One hundred and fifty. And with the crowd yelling encouragement, TWO HUNDRED sit-ups.

At 25 cents each, with 42 sponsors from the staff, Sandy that morning raised $2,100 for the hospice campaign!

And just as importantly, her creative approach opened other people's minds to ways they might help. Jennifer decided to organize a Friday bake-sale in the staff room, with proceeds directed to the campaign. Jeremy put together a small group to organize a staff-wide car wash. And Candace, who knew several masseuses, persuaded them to donate several one-hour sessions for which Candace held a silent auction.

In the end, Sandy did much more than firm up her abs and raise money for the hospice. She served as a model and an inspiration for others to participate as well.

STEP 9

Get the Word Out

By this point in your campaign, if all has gone well, you've raised 75 percent or even as much as 90 percent of your goal. Those most closely tied to your project have made their gifts.

In the early stages, small gifts didn't seem terribly important. But once you have the bulk of the money in hand, and all of your prospects for larger gifts have been approached, even smaller gifts become significant – if you hope to reach your goal, that is.

It's time now to broadcast your success in every way possible – to reach as many people as possible and to bring your campaign to a rousing conclusion.

■ The bigger the splash the better

The Community Market campaign I spoke of earlier had raised all but $60,000 of its $1.2 million goal. While that isn't a lot relative to the target, it gave Rosalyn, the campaign director, her chance to achieve another objective: Making sure *everyone* who shopped at the Market had a chance to participate.

Rosalyn knew that to finish the campaign she'd need lots of small gifts. She also knew that by expanding the pool of donors, she'd be able to strengthen the connection between shoppers and the Market – a bond that could prove invaluable if sometime in the future the Market needed to raise money for its operating budget.

So this canny campaign director set about finding a way to engage the entire community. Rosalyn began by enlisting Laura, who was in charge of communications for a local bank. She hoped Laura would help her figure out how to get their local newspaper to cover the campaign.

Knowing that newspapers aren't especially interested in fundraising –those tired photos of oversized checks just don't interest today's audiences – Rosalyn and Laura conceived of a different approach.

They outlined seven stories about the Community Market – one for each section of the paper. Each story presented the Market in a different light. For example, a local elementary school class would do an art project on the Market – good fodder for the Community section. New Market merchants would be interviewed for the business section. And pre-arranged tours of the Market were listed in the Calendar.

The idea was to create a Market theme throughout the paper, led off by a big headline about the renovation plans and the fundraising progress.

Laura presented this entire package of stories to the editor. To make the idea more appealing, the Market campaign agreed to purchase an ad on the day the stories were to run.

The editor approved and the newspaper blitz started the week before Easter, the busiest Market week of the year.

With the publicity in full swing, Rosalyn and her committee practically camped out at the Market and capitalized in every way they could.

They adorned the area with banners and photos. Periodically, they raffled off silk-screened shopping bags to people who put $20 or more in a campaign collection jug.

Volunteers wore tomato and chicken costumes, and roamed the aisles encouraging people to visit the campaign stand where they could give cash, pick up an "I Love Market/I Gave" button, sign up for the raffle, and learn about the renovations.

Kids walking by the stand were delighted to get orange plastic pens shaped like carrots. And a very large meat thermometer showed the progress of the campaign with a red dial and arrow that moved throughout the three days from rare to medium to well-done.

Over the course of these three days, this broad-based campaign garnered hundreds of well-wishers and donors. Again and again, shoppers stopped by to say how important the Market was to them and to thank the volunteers for their efforts. People gave pennies and dollars and hundreds of dollars and they recounted their Market stories, many going back to when they were children.

When all was said and done, the three days raised $15,000. In the larger fundraising scheme, it wasn't much money, and it left more money to raise. But the energy and excitement generated, in combination with the assorted media coverage, set the stage for taking the campaign over goal with a final push to bring in gifts from donors who had put off making their decision.

■ All the world's a stage

Among the more creative events I ever saw for getting the word out was for a new hospital for women and babies. Most of the money had been raised and the building was nearing completion. The campaign committee decided to give community leaders and the press a preview of the new facility with an early-morning event.

Using the unfinished lobby of the new building as a backdrop, a talented local actress performed a short piece in which, with the help of a few simple props – hair ribbons, a silk scarf, and a cane – she transformed herself through every stage of life, weaving in a story about how the new facility would be there for her.

It was fun, it was inventive, and it caught the substance and spirit of the project and the campaign. The hospital might well have opted for a more traditional black-tie event, but I suspect this shorter, less expensive, more creative approach generated more attention in the media and through word of mouth.

■ In praise of "late" donors

Some donors prefer to give late in the campaign. Perhaps they're the same people who arrive late for events or for dinner. I'm not sure. My guess is that the urgency of the last moment particularly inspires them.

Sheepishly I admit to being like that.

I recently gave $1,000 to an organization I work with. This group's goal was to raise $1 million and, nearing the end of their campaign, they still had $50,000 to go.

A FAIL-PROOF GUIDE

In terms of the goal, my check wasn't a big one. Many people had given much larger sums. But $1000 is significant to me, and I wrestled with sending that much. The stock market was crumbling, my husband had retired, and the cause wasn't a priority for me. In fact, I wondered if I should be giving anything at all.

Still, it was a campaign I was involved with and I knew I'd feel bad if I didn't give at all. So, despite my misgivings, I made the gift. I felt that $1000 would put me at a level I could live with, and that given the $50,000 left to raise, it would still make a real difference.

A few days later, I got an email from the director thanking me. The campaign had reached its goal and might even go over! Although my gift played only a small part, it was still emotionally satisfying to think I had helped close the gap. I was happy I'd sent the check. And the director's prompt and warm response increased the chances I'll give again later.

So particularly when the finish line is near, let people know you're close to the goal and that *they* can help push you over. I suspect many of us like to be finish-line heroes.

■ Love 'em if they give and love 'em if they don't

When you've devoted yourself to a campaign, and

lived and breathed it for months, it's easy to lose perspective and to think everyone *should* give. "Don't these skinflints see the importance of what we're doing!?"

But ultimately, that attitude is poisonous – for you, for the campaign, and for your organization's relationships. Remember, most of us struggle with balancing the desire to give *and* the desire to hang on to what we have.

It's your job to ask; it's *their* job to say "yes" or "no." If the asking comes as an invitation rather than a moral judgment, it'll spread goodwill – for your cause, for this campaign, and for the others that will someday follow.

At dinner the other night, I sat next to Jenny, a woman who manages her own small foundation. When I asked how she dealt with so many requests, she told me she finds it hard to say "no."

Very often people become indignant when she turns them down, writing nasty letters or even calling to complain. In turn that makes Jenny angry, irritated, and cynical – not qualities she likes in herself. "Who are they," she said, "to tell me what I *should* be giving to?"

But Jenny also related a good experience. After being turned down, a woman called to *thank* Jenny for considering her request and to ask for suggestions about making her future proposals stronger.

The call encouraged Jenny to review the request again and make some suggestions. And in doing so, Jenny became a partner rather than just a short-term funder. "She didn't criticize me," Jenny told me. "She understood that even my resources are limited. And her understanding made me want to support her."

I suspect that this new partnership may yield far more for the solicitor than a simple check.

The next time you or one of your committee members are turned down, keep in mind that often it has nothing to do with you or your cause. Maybe the timing is poor, maybe resources are stretched, maybe an unexpected expense has reared its head.

If *you* were in a position where you had to say "no," even when your heart wanted to say "yes," what you'd want is to be understood, not criticized. It's that very kind of compassion that will lead you to support the cause when your personal circumstances change.

STEP 10

Thank Those Who Helped and Those Who Gave

Champagne. Roses. Handshakes. Heartfelt notes. And sometimes even extraordinary gifts like the cornerstone I mentioned earlier. These are the gestures that conclude a campaign.

For three years, Becky, a board member of a community hospital in Pennsylvania had worked tirelessly on raising money for a new wing. She had given her life to the project, often to the dismay of her husband who was happily retired and wondered why his wife no longer had time for him.

Largely through Becky's efforts, the hospital raised more money than anyone thought possible. So when the campaign drew to a close and the building was under construction, the board decided to honor Becky and her long-suffering husband. They anteed up the money themselves and sent the pair on an all expenses paid trip to Rome, a place Becky and Joe had talked about going for years. This was a board of hard-nosed businessmen who ran a very successful hospital. Never would Becky have imagined they'd appreciate her work so extravagantly.

The big gift to Becky was remarkable. But equally moving was the notebook of letters sent to Denise, who funded an elementary school music program. Each letter was written by a third grader and described what he or she loved about music. Each was decorated with drawings and musical symbols they had learned.

Not once, but several times over the next few months when I visited Denise, she pulled out her book and showed me another letter that had particularly touched her heart.

Molly, the development director of a social justice organization in New York, used a small party with funny awards to recognize her volunteers. She thought hard about what each person had done well and came up with a fitting tribute for each.

Clark, for example, got the Call Master Award for having made the most calls. Sylvie got the Rookie Award since it was her first time asking for gifts. Steve got the Golden Globe for having brought in the most money.

Molly cajoled the executive director into presenting the certificates (which she printed out on her Epson) at a special meeting. He read each one quite seriously and presented them graduation-style. The next day, Molly sent a list of the awards to the board along with a full report of the campaign's success.

And a funny thing happened. Before the week was out, Molly was fielding calls from people asking if they could help with the next fundraising effort. Wow!

Thanking people doesn't have to be big or lavish or expensive. It has to be *authentic*. Often it's the small, real gestures that matter most.

■ Gratification that counts

But certificates and recognition notwithstanding, I've learned over the years that for the people who drive the fundraising process, working doggedly from beginning to end, the public hoopla and celebration marking the campaign's end has surprisingly little effect on them.

When I called Jim, the founder of the Science Factory you met in Step 1, and asked how he felt at the very moment he raised the millionth dollar, here's what he said. "Was I elated when we went over goal?

Well, I guess there was a moment. But then I had the overwhelming sense that raising a million dollars was merely another step in a much bigger challenge. We'd built an airplane. But now we had to make it fly. And once in the air, we had to know where we wanted it to go."

Jim continued: "But it *was* thrilling to see the community believe in our idea. And it was thrilling to meet so many selfless people during the campaign. And it continues to be thrilling to hear a fifth grader shout with wonder and joy in the Science Factory – there's no greater high than that. The fundraising was just money."

Jim's comments reflect the way many people feel when they finish a large campaign. There is the satisfaction that comes from raising the money. But the lasting reward is the realization that one has accomplished something that makes a difference in the lives of others.

I'm grateful to Jim and the many other people like Kim and Carole and Rosalyn and Jeanne whose stories have made this book possible. These people dive right in. They work through thick and thin to make the most out of what they have in order to build something that will make the world a better place.

I suspect that describes you, too; you wouldn't be

reading this book otherwise. You're precious in today's world – a caring individual who's willing to put in the hours because your cause, whether it involves health or education or culture, is important. Many depend on you for their well-being, if not their very lives.

I hope in my small way I've helped to build your confidence – you already have the courage. Now it's time for you to go out and raise the money and, as Steve Jobs would say, "Put a ding in the universe."

AFTERWORD

So how long will it take to raise $1 million, you may be wondering.

My friend and colleague Bob Pierpont, who through his long career as a fundraiser and consultant guided many campaigns, has told me again and again: "A campaign is no more and no less than a dollar goal up against a deadline."

I've talked lots in this book about dollar goals, but you'll also need timetables and deadlines to drive you from one step to another until you get through all 10 steps.

Just how long will it take to raise $1 million depends on whether you already have strong relationships with those who'll be able to make the large gifts.

Remember Pete who walked in with a million dollar check? Pete had worked as a program volunteer for years before he made that gift. So while the gift seemed out of the blue, in reality it was deeply rooted in a trusting and collaborative relationship built over time.

If you've already established such relationships, and people are passionate, informed, and committed to your project, you may be able to raise $1 million or more in a year or 18 months. But if you're like most organizations that have one or two major donors already engaged but many more relationships to develop, it will take longer, sometimes much longer. You'll be wise to allow at least two and perhaps three or even four years from beginning to end.

Some organizations have timetables imposed on them. The lease on their building is expiring and can't be renewed. That was the case with Rich's charter school I mentioned in Step 7. And, yes, a forced timetable, like a forced march, pushes people to function on fast forward. But beware, if your major donors aren't already involved, your need to move fast may mean little to them.

Other organizations must create artificial timetables to keep the project on track. Some rely on a strategic plan adopted by the board. Others might find a challenge grant that delineates a timeframe. Still others have strong leaders who through sheer force of will create a sense of urgency that keeps the campaign on everyone's front burner.

But whether your timetable is imposed from the inside or from without, you'll need deadlines to discipline your forward momentum through all 10 steps. Without them, as Martin Luther cautioned, "How soon 'not now' becomes 'never'."

ABOUT THE AUTHOR

Andrea Kihlstedt is fascinated by what makes people tick. She has spent the last 27 years as a capital campaign consultant, working with organizations large and small, giving her ample opportunities to observe remarkable people who through their courage, commitment, and energies make our world a better place through fundraising.

Andrea's book, *Capital Campaigns: Strategies that Work*, now in its third edition, has become a primary resource for fundraisers and consultants. It discusses in great detail the structures and systems that help move the campaign process ahead and includes a CD with downloadable material and samples you can adapt for your organization.

Andrea has recently launched www.AskingMatters.com, a website designed to provide tools that inform, support and motivate people to go out and ask for gifts.

Andrea lives in New York City with her husband, Tyko.

GRATITUDE

Thanking people is one of my great pleasures as it reminds me of the many gifts I have received.

I thank Ralph Goodno, Terry Nolan, Rich Berlin, Xan Blake and Charlie Trautmann for giving me the opportunity to watch great leaders at work.

I thank Carol Golden and Carole Haas Gravagno, and Kim Oxholm for the opportunity to get to know people who are committed and generous, and who follow through.

I thank Rosalyn Ward for showing me again and again how good will and good humor win the day.

I give a special thanks to Jim Bunting whose monumental determination, clear thinking and swing-for-the-fences approach inspire me to do more than I might.

I thank Jezra Kaye and Jerry Ciancolo for their work on this book. Every writer should be so fortunate to have editors and friends like these two. They make me sound far better than I am.

I thank Jerold Panas, philanthropy's preeminent writer, for his constructive suggestions.

And finally, I thank my wonderful women friends of many years – Barbara, Maria, Carol and Heike. I know you are there.

The list of people I wish to thank is very long and this page very small. My heartfelt thanks to all of those people who inspire me and hold my hand along the way.

1-Hour Board Books from Emerson & Church

The Ultimate Board Member's Book
Kay Sprinkel Grace, 111 pp., $24.95

Here is a book for *all* board members:
• Those needing an orientation to the unique responsibilities of a nonprofit board,
• Those wishing to clarify exactly what their individual role is,
• Those hoping to fulfill their charge with maximum effectiveness.

Kay Sprinkel Grace's perceptive work will take board members just one hour to read, and yet they'll come away from *The Ultimate Board Member's Book* with a firm command of just what they need to do to help their organization succeed.

It's all here in 111 jargon-free pages: how boards work, what the job entails, the time commitment involved, the role of staff, serving on committees and task forces, fundraising responsibilities, conflicts of interest, group decision-making, effective recruiting, de-enlisting board members, board self-evaluation, and more.

The Fundraising Habits of Supremely Successful Boards
Jerold Panas, 108 pp., $24.95

Over the course of a storied career, Jerold Panas has worked with literally thousands of boards, from those governing the toniest of prep schools to those spearheading the local Y. He has counseled floundering groups; he has been the wind beneath the wings of boards whose organizations have soared.

In fact, it's a safe bet that Panas has observed more boards at work than perhaps anyone in America, all the while helping them to surpass their campaign goals of $100,000 to $100 million.

Funnel every ounce of that experience and wisdom into a single book and what you end up with is *The Fundraising Habits of Supremely Successful Boards*, the brilliant culmination of what Panas has learned firsthand about boards who excel at the task of resource development.

Fundraising Habits offers a panoply of habits any board would be wise to cultivate. Some are specific, with measurable outcomes. Others are more intangible, with Panas seeking to impart an attitude of success.

1-Hour Board Books from Emerson & Church

Big Gifts for Small Groups
Andy Robinson, 104 pp., $24.95

If yours is among the tens of thousands of organizations for whom six- and seven-figure gifts are unattainable, then Andy Robinson's book, *Big Gifts for Small Groups*, is an ideal choice for you and your board.

Robinson is the straightest of shooters; there literally isn't one piece of advice in this book that's glib or inauthentic. And as a result of Robinson's 'no bull' style, board members will instantly take to the book.

They'll learn everything they need to know about soliciting gifts in the $500 to $5,000 range: how to get ready for the campaign, whom to approach, where to find them, where to conduct the meeting, what to bring, how to ask, how to make it easy for the donor to give, what to do once you have the commitment – even how to convey thanks in a memorable way.

Great Boards for Small Groups
Andy Robinson, 110 pp., $24.95

Yours is a good board, but you want it to be better. You want:
• Clearly defined objectives
• Meetings with more focus
• Broader participation in fundraising, and
• More follow-through between meetings

You want these and a dozen other tangibles and intangibles that will propel your board from good to great. Say hello to your guide, Andy Robinson, a pragmatist par excellence.

Over the past 20 years, as a board member, volunteer and consultant, Robinson has put into practice what he preaches. Not only does he stand unshakably behind his advice, he has a real knack for offering "forehead-slapping" solutions.

In addition to chapters on everything from orientation to board/staff relations, Robinson homes in on specific problems such as poorly attended meetings, spotty follow-through, inactive board members, conflicts of interest, weak agendas, and much more.

1-Hour Board Books from Emerson & Church

The 11 Questions Every Donor Asks
Harvey McKinnon, 104 pp., $24.95

In what it sets out to do, *The 11 Questions* is deceptively simple. Harvey McKinnon wants merely to prepare you – whether you're a board member, volunteer, or staff – for the questions you'll inevitably face from prospective donors, spoken or not.

McKinnon has identified 11 such questions, ranging from "Why me?" to "Will my gift make a difference?" to "Will I have a say over how you use my gift?" And rather than dryly tell you to "Do this" or "Do that," the author punctuates his prose with dramatic real-life stories. They're highly engaging, each one skillfully selected to drive home a point.

Jerold Panas calls *The 11 Questions* "A beautifully polished gem, with real-life stories that unerringly hit their mark."

Fundraising Mistakes that Bedevil All Boards (and Staff Too)
Kay Sprinkel Grace, 110 pp., $24.95

Over the past 70 years, organizations have tested literally hundreds of fundraising techniques and strategies.

Some have succeeded beyond expectation – billion dollar capital campaigns attest to that – but too many approaches have failed.

Yet, strangely enough, many of these unsuccessful methods, because they seem commonsensical, are repeated to this day. Over and over again.

The result? Untold hours are wasted, causes go unfunded, and disappointment and frustration demoralize volunteers and staff everywhere.

If your board members and volunteers scrupulously avoid the 44 time and money wasters explored in this illuminating book, they'll dramatically sharpen their fundraising skills and enter each campaign – whether annual or capital – primed for success.

Copies of this and other books from the
publisher are available at discount when
purchased in quantity for boards of directors
or staff. Call 508-359-0019 or visit
www.emersonandchurch.com

Emerson
& Church
PUBLISHERS